Steel Valley Elegy

Steel Valley Elegy

Poems by

William Heath

Cover design by Shay Culligan

ISBN: 978-1-63980-103-9

Kelsay Books
502 South 1040 East, A-119
American Fork, Utah 84003
Kelsaybooks.com

Once again, for Roser

Dust we shall be, but dust in love

Special thanks to Frank and Holly Bergon, Zeese Popanikolas,
David Salner, and Hope Maxwell Snyder
for their valuable suggestions.

Acknowledgments

American Journal of Poetry: "Guru Marajah Ji," "The Banality of Evil"

Appalachian Journal: "The Wind," "Tornado"

Approaches: "Nightwatch"

Avatar Review: "The Love Songs of Frogs"

Awake in the World, Vol. II: "Skeleton in the Woods"

Cathexis Northwest: "Crime Scene"

Change Seven: "Key West"

College English: "You Numbskull"

Concho River Review: "Campus Wisdom," "Jury Duty"

Cutthroat: "The Cottonmouth in the Outhouse"

The Dead Mule School of Southern Literature: "Gator," "Southern Belle"

Deep South: "The Delta," "The Town," "The Mansion," "A Lynching in Mississippi"

Free State Review: "Dock of the Bay"

MacQueen's Quinterly: "Louis' Basque Corner"

Mantis: A Journal of Poetry: "The Corner," "Postmodern Poetry"

Mid-Atlantic Review: "How I Left the War and Took Up Basketball"

Mudlark: "Bread Loaf: Two Views"

Night Moves in Ohio (Finishing Line Press 2019), a chapbook: "Steel Valley Elegy," "My Father Put the Shot," "Skipping Stones," "High Jumper," "A Hit in Shaker Heights," "I Beat Dolph," "The Green Man," "The Girls from Campbell," "An Inside Job," "Mom's Final Days," "Milking Time," "Guts and Glory," "The Raft"

North Dakota Quarterly: "The Hough Riots," "Active Shooter," "A Life More Abundant," "Prospecting"

Northern Virginia Revew: "Entropy"

Orchards Poetry Journal, "Winslow Homer's *The Fog Warning*"

Patterson Literary Review: "Our Black Sheep"

Pennsylvania Literary Review: "Woodstock," "Tripping"
Poetry Leaves V: "Raking Leaves"
Poetry Now: "Night Moves in Ohio"
Quadrant: "Intimations," "Americana"
Running with Water: "Pledge Night"
The Sandy River Review: "The Shack"
Streetlight Magazine: "The Cold War in Poland (Ohio)"
Tipton Poetry Journal: "Fascist Kitsch"
Umbrella Factory Magazine, "Honky-Tonk," "Swift Creek,"
    "On Suicide"
Welter: "The Nightingale's Song"
What Rough Beast: "Urban Renewal in Detroit"

Contents

III Intimations

I

Night Moves in Ohio

Steel Valley Elegy

I speak Steel Valley American. Once mills
lined the Mahoning River from Youngstown
Sheet and Tube's Jeannette Blast Furnace
on Brier Hill to Republic Steel in Struthers.
Coal intensified to coke turned iron ore
into molten ingots that were rolled into slabs,
scarfed free of impurities, shaped for strength:
bridges to span waters, girders for skyscrapers,
tanks, ships, guns, and shells to win World War II,
machines and factories for our bounty.

The workers—Honkies from Smokey Hollow,
Slovaks from Nebo, Dagos, Polacks, Blacks—
dress for combat: hard hats, safety glasses,
asbestos coats, steel-toed boots. Beware
of breathing tainted air. Openhearth blast
furnaces singe eyebrows, sear lungs, "pants
on fire" no metaphor. At the last whistle
dehydrated men head for the taverns
on tap at each plant gate, down boilermakers
(a shot of whiskey dropped in a mug of beer),
cash checks, play the "bug," stagger home.

Men make serious money making steel.
A house with a lawn, a Ford or Chevy
in the drive. Soot on windows means food
on the table. Mills create the weather:
skies dark in daytime, bright at night; clothes
hang in the cellar to avoid black rain.
The city is called "Little Chicago," eighty-
five bombings—"Youngstown tune-ups"—

as Cleveland and Pittsburgh mobsters blow
each other apart for control of the bug
and other games of chance. Barbers charge
five bucks for a haircut, ten to start your car.

Crossing the bridge into town I see
the Valley of Ashes in *The Great Gatsby:*
grey heaps of slag, bins of scrap metal,
the fuming rusty-orange sulfurous river
that might ignite at the flip of a match;
low, corrugated buildings topped by tall
towers and vent stacks burn off waste gas;
serpentine trains shunted into sideyards,
scotched into freight cars, unloaded one by one.

My Czech girlfriend, whose father works in steel,
spreads a blanket in her backyard above the valley.
As evening falls the infernal glow of the mills
becomes magical. Yellow flames from smelters
make air-borne soot sparkle, blotting out the stars.
White-hot slabs glide down conveyor belts.
The screeching, clanging industrial din
has a percussive rhythm. Teens in love,
for all we know our kisses last hours.
Now the mills are gone. The only people left
misplaced their car keys—still I celebrate
the steel valley's brutal lost beauty.

Our Black Sheep

was Uncle Frank, grandfather's brother.
First arrested for theft at fourteen,
when he was twenty-one he did time
for stealing muskrat and skunk skins.
Once near Oberlin he fell into a stupor
at an Erie Lackawanna line crossing.
The speeding train, no time to toot,
whisked his horse to greener pastures,
leaving Frank and buggy unscathed.
Deaf to his mother's pleas he played
his favorite, "All By Myself," endlessly
on the Victrola. One drunken night
driving home in his Model T Ford,
he sheered off three telephone poles,
finally stopped by smacking the side
of the house. Next morning my dad
went out to inspect the damage.
The poles, cut away at ground level,
still dangled from sagging wires.
Each severed pole had swung up,
clearing the way for the car
to hit the next. Everyone agreed
Uncle Frank led a charmed life,
until his liver gave out. Dad,
who never touched a drop of
the creature, helped carry the coffin.
They buried Frank on Butternut Ridge,
yonder from grandfather's farm.

My Father Put the Shot

In the photo he stands
in track shorts and top,
hands clasped behind his back
to accentuate his biceps.
The "O" on his broad chest
was proof he put the shot
for the Oberlin track team.
A farmer's son, he worked
hard as a boy, putting
the shot just one more
form of tossing rocks out
of a ploughed cornfield.

After graduation he taught
chemistry in a rural school.
He loved to tell the tale of how
a bully, gripping his desk
screwed to the floor, ignored
an order to leave the class.
My father jerked the desk
into the air and tossed it
and the bully out the door.
The next day the lad came back
with his much larger father.
"Did you throw my boy out of class?"
he demanded and Dad replied,
"Yes, I did." "Did he deserve it?"
"Yes, he did." "Well, if he acts up
again, beat the hell out of him,"
he said, shaking Dad's hand
and smacking his son on the head
for good measure.

Feats like these
get a man promoted to principal.
His office at Hays Junior High
in Youngstown had a drawer full
of confiscated weapons—switch-
blades, clubs, even a zip gun
wrapped in black tape.
He enforced discipline by swats
from a perforated paddle hung
on the wall behind his desk.

Perhaps that's why he only hit
me twice in his life—once for
filching a neighbor boy's toy
truck and bulldozer, and then
for faking a bicycle accident,
enhanced by my ketchup-
covered body, beside the highway.
He used his belt and, his voice
breaking, admonished, "Don't ever
make me have to do that again."

Skipping Stones

What boy, with a stream
pooling nearby to form
a neat swimming hole,
didn't? The trick is
smooth flat ones, circular
to fit the curve of an index
finger. A sidearm toss
with a final flick of the wrist
gives the stone the proper
spin to skim the surface,
and skip, skip, skip, skip again
before it suddenly sinks.
It takes a keen eye to spot
the best prospects, strength
and skill for a perfect throw,
and then, by god, the stone
takes on a grace, a kind of joy
as each airborne leap breaks
free of the law of gravity
to fly for a moment—until
the water claims its own.

Ballad of K. K. Granger

If I did this dry, what couldn't I do wet.
—Don Quijote

In a corner of Ohio
whose name I don't care to recall,
there lives an ambitious boy
who devours so many books
his head is filled with dreams
of earthly fame. But the town
already has its own knight errant,
Mr. Granger by name, he rides
his nag Rocky down Main Street,
a flyboy's cap on his noggin,
a rooster under his arm.

How he gets that way is tragic:
in the last days of World War II
his only daughter, who lives
with him, learns a landmine
had cost her husband his legs.
Mr. Granger finds her hanging
in the closet, is unhinged by
her death. Sheet & Tube lets
him go, he brings his desk
and chair home in revenge,
for years never leaves his house.

After his prim and proper wife
passes away, he rides Rocky,
ribs on display beneath a mangy
brown and white hide, for grub
at Schwartz's store, a Cola
at Islay's ice cream parlor.
He has gray hair, sunken cheeks,
false teeth; even in summer

he wears layers of long-sleeved
cotton and flannel shirts,
baggy pants on a tight belt.
He lives on a circle of fine homes
known as the town Manor,
his garage, Rocky's stable,
not a rarely mucked-out stall
nor the seldom-cleaned house
smells sweetly of amber.
Many a day he goes riding
down paths in the nearby forest,
anything found of interest
he tucks under his shirt
to show to us curious kids.

Could be an owl, another time
baby raccoons, you never know
what critter might next make
its debut—a frog, a snake,
chipmunks, birds, kittens.
Once he offers to share
a raccoon sandwich, swears
it is delicious, he's roasted
the meat himself. Did *he*
kill the raccoon, I wonder,
or find it dead in the woods.

His nature is good-hearted,
he loves animals and does odd
jobs for people whether or not
they want them done. Once he
puts a pregnant dog in a neighbor's
living room so she can be

comfortable having her puppies
on the couch. Several small bags
hang from his saddle, one with
candy for children, but what
secrets are in the others?

On Memorial Day he rides
at the front of the parade
decked out in Civil War blue,
holding aloft a makeshift sword.
Then there is the time he leads
Rocky into the gym, lets loose
a rooster at a PTA gabfest.
Why would he do that?
People in our town assume
God's ways are not ours,
no point in squawking about it.

How I Left the War
and Took Up Basketball

The first time he whipped
a behind-the-back pass
to the open man on his blind side
Bob Cousy knew he was a star.
A small man with big hands
quick as a poet his pin-point passes
scored baskets.

Me, I practiced down in our pitch-black
cement cellar, dribbling with either hand
in the dark. Sometimes I sat with my eyes shut,
spinning the ball on my fingers, rubbing
the nubbles and whispering to myself.

This was near the end of the Ohio phase
of the Korean War when coming home
at dusk from the Battle of Hidden Valley
and Lee Run Creek I ran head-first
into a barbed wire fence slicing my skin
at the hairline. My mother screamed to see
the web of blood while I searched my skull
in the mirror praying for a scar.

At first I shot from the hip, pushing off
on my left leg to launch a giant step up
with my right, banking the ball off the board
to drop through the hoop. By junior high
I had a fallaway jump shot and basketballs
on the brain.

Paperboy

My predecessor coasts
too fast down a driveway
and out onto the road
where a speeding car
takes his life. His body
is gone by the time
I get there but I see
the blood on his bike,
front wheel spinning,
papers strewn in a ditch,
one shoe. Nonetheless
I take the job, the pay
isn't much, I hate
getting up so early,
some houses have dogs
snapping at my legs,
yet I get fringe benefits.

Squeezing a pair of pliers
from my back pocket
the wire girding the stack
snaps back and the papers
fluff up as if in relief.
I pack them best I can
in my handlebar basket,
peddle off on my route
that always features
the thirty-something lady—
lustrous hair piled high,
diaphanous pink negligee,
Janet-Leigh-like shape—
greeting me each morning
on her front porch.
I suppose, I guess,

as I would have said
back then, the offer
is there, but I am
just a boy, mumbling
in reply to her thanks,
"You're welcome, ma'am."

The Cold War in Poland (Ohio)

In school we learn to lie down
in the face of Evil from the skies.
"Take cover," the first commandment
during air-raid drills as we duck
under our desks, then "All clear."
No one dares to say that with
or without these precautions,
if a bomb fell, we'll all be toast.

All day we wait on edges of seats
for firehouse sirens to sound the alarm.
Part of the Civil Defense system,
we Boy Scouts chop trees,
clear brush for a circular space
deep in the Poland woods, use
the logs for an observation tower
where our trusty binoculars scan
Ohio heavens for Soviet planes.

One family across the street digs
a fallout shelter in their backyard,
complete with a *No Trespassing* sign,
little realizing they are complicit
to their own burial—leaving fewer
unsightly bodies lying around—
because if the initial blast doesn't
get you the radiation will.

                  As luck
would have it, nearby Youngstown
with its thriving steel mills is
a strategic target, not us—our destiny
is to be collateral damage.

A Hit in Shaker Heights

30 October 1959

I am seventeen, visiting
my cousin in Shaker Heights, posh
suburb of Cleveland where bad things
rarely happen. On Scottsdale Boulevard
a yellow sash across a driveway, boys
being boys we want to know what
the fuss is about. Between the garage
and the house a pool of blood, chalk
outlines of a body, a gun, a knife.
A woman comes with a garden hose,
washes the blood down a drain.

I am from Poland, suburb of mobbed-up
Youngstown, juicy bone of contention
between Cleveland and Pittsburgh for control
of vending machines, juke boxes, the bug,
gambling, prostitution, hard drugs.
Bombings are commonplace, murders
no rarity. This, my first crime scene.
Mike Sperazzo was shot from ambush.
He'd done time for armed robbery, fencing
stolen property; he was a bookie,
played the horses, bankrolled floating
crap games. Maybe the hit was to settle
a score, or a mob boss gave the word.

What haunts me is that his wife
heard the car pull in, out the window
saw a man by the hedge fire twice,
slip away, return. The killer stepped
on Mike's chest for the coup de grâce.
Did she rush out of the house to see
if he was dead, then call the police?

When we arrive, cop cars and reporters
are gone. She is alone in the house,
a Mafia wife who hoses her husband's
blood, pooled beside the chalk outline
of his body, down the driveway drain.

High Jumper

I place black tape
on my bedroom wall
at six feet, my height,
for hours I imagine
if it were a crossbar
how I could clear it.
I am a high jumper
with a telltale
bounce in my stride
and in those days
a leap like that breaks
the school record.
The Western Roll
is my style, first
a giant kick up
with my right leg,
a quick midair twist
to place my belly
above the bar,
then a backwards kick
with my left leg
before I smack down
in the sawdust pit
and look up to see
the jump is mine.

I Beat Dolph

Dolph Shayes's basketball camp
is in the Upper Adirondacks
near Plattsburg, New York.
The summer before my senior year
I go there for two weeks.
He is the best foul shooter
in the NBA, his long set shot,
well before the three-point rule,
a lethal wonder. He takes fifty
foul shots each week, swishing
at least 45. Top that, you get
a red patch with white letters,
"I beat Dolph." Third time around
I hit 47, claim my reward.

Each cabin forms a team
in an ongoing tournament.
Our tallest player Tommy Piper
is heir to the Piper Cub we all
long to fly one wealthy day.
As point guard, the offense flows
through me, but in the first half
of the championship game, I am
called for five fouls and ejected.
Weeping tears of baffled rage
I stomp off the court, certain
I have cost my guys the trophy
we were sure we'd win. Instead
of sitting on the bench I run
to the woods, circle the lake,
come back to my cabin at dusk.

Coach, waiting on my bunk,
says he is ashamed of me,
I should have stayed at the court,
rooted for our players, who,
to my astonishment, win
without me. Next day Dolph
reminds me that basketball
is a team game. A point guard
should know that. I am blinded,
not the last time, by my ego.
I am not indispensable.

My coach, I learn, during
the 1950s point-shaving scandal,
took the fall for CCNY's famous
head coach, and lost his career.
Dolph knew the true story,
hired him for his camp.
He taught me good sportsmanship,
and the topsy-turvy way
a gentleman folds his pants:
first align the cuffs, then
slide them on the hanger.

Night Moves in Ohio

A blow job at the drive-in,
an empty bottle of Deep
Ruby Fruity Native tossed
in the back seat, so drunk
they drive off forgetting
to replace the speaker.
When it rips out they both
giggle and he steps
on the gas, knocking
the attendant on his ass,
splattering gravel to the highway,
peeling rubber twenty feet
down the road, heading
for the strip-mine quarries
to shake off the cops.

Still giggling they fumble
off their clothes: he trying
to bite her bra in two,
she squeezing his nuts.
Stripped to the buff they
stumble down to the water
and go skinny-dipping,
laughing so hard they damn
near swallow the pond.
Nobody drowns. A few years
later he comes home from college
and she is a social worker.
They went parking but he
can't get it up when she
goes down on him. Furious,
she tears off and totals
her Chevy in a ditch.

The Green Man

"Print the legend"

As a boy he climbed up
a utility pole to retrieve
a bird's nest. He heard
the hot lines singing,
then his face brushed
high-tension and the shock
melted it. The one eye
that survived slid down
a pink cheek. The full nose
drained to small red holes.
His mouth was a black
breathing scar. Too sensitive
to ever see the sun again,
at night the Green Man
walks the back roads
of western Pennsylvania
between New Galilee
and Kopple until the word
spreads. One summer night
we pack six in a car
to catch a glimpse of that
incredible face in the glare
of our headlights. The sight
is electrifying. On cue,
the girls scream in terror,
we kiss away their fear.
The cops, true to custom,
are quick to pounce
on the anticipated U-turn.
They flash us down, beams
stab at startled faces.
We follow them to a house,

wait for the sun to rise
so the Justice of the Peace
can impose a handsome fine
to support the town. Warned
and released we race back
to Poland, Ohio, talking much
louder than usual, trying
to laugh away that face.

The Girls from Campbell

No sooner do we unload
the cars and select our beds
at the Lake Erie summer cottage
we seniors are renting for a week
than the girls from Campbell
barge in the door, wearing
tight T-shirts and short shorts,
head straight to the fridge,
pop tops, start chugging.
One girl asks where we live.
When I say "Poland" she shakes
a wrist to show how rich we are.
Campbell for us conjures up
steel mills along the Mahoning,
the all-Black basketball team
we beat in the tournament,
and shady dealings of the Mafiosi
operating out of Youngstown.

A few beer cases later. One of
the Campbell girls has passed out
in the bedroom while necking
with Bob, who, when he notices
no response, asks for our help.
What to do? We splash water
on her face, walk her around
the room, but all she mumbles,
repeatedly, is "Fuck Butchy,"
her no good boyfriend we're told.
At this point it is past midnight,
the problem is how to sneak
the plastered girl past the chaperone
asleep on the couch by the television.

Our solution, carry her over to
their nearby cabin, slide her in
the back window of a bedroom,
the only sound her Butchy mantra.
When we awake the next morning
the girls from Campbell are gone
and our fridge is bare. Perhaps
there is a moral here, but it
eludes the guys from Poland.

Pledge Night

for Rich Pejeau

We think of everything.
Ramshackle abandoned house
lost in undergrowth, rumor

has it that a couple has died
in a car crash, no relatives,
everything just as it was

when they left. Dirty dishes
in the sink, beds unmade,
stench from the garbage like

you wouldn't believe. Careful
to preserve the cobwebs, strings
tied to doors that creaked,

someone in hiding to ping
the piano when the time
comes. Best of all the preserved

head stolen from science lab
prominent on the pillow,
blankets shaped like a body

under the bedspread. Blind-
folded pledges driven around,
snuck the back way to the cellar—

that is the plan. We choose Rich
to be our test case, give him
a tiny flashlight, tell him there

is something in the bedroom
we want him to go see.
We are sure we can smell

his fear. Reluctantly he goes
up the stairs, at the first floor
the piano pings on schedule,

a door creaks, a cobweb
brushes across his eyes,
the wind whistles through

a window open a crack.
On the second floor, he
steps into the dark room,

his pencil-thin light shines
on the bed:—gray strands of hair
on the pillow, the ghoulish

face drained of flesh, eyes like
dried raisins, yellow teeth
in a wide mirthless grin—

and says, "Oh, Hello."

Guts and Glory

You bet I've got guts, I survived
high school for Christ's sake.
Nobody bullied me to jump off
the high board or chug a case
of Rolling Rock, let alone smoke
one more joint, my scalp tingling
enough as it was. In spite of guys
egging me on from the back seat
I never exceed the speed limit
by more than twenty miles—when
a cop pulls me over it is for
running a stop sign I didn't see.
I need glasses. I learn that
at my physical for Vietnam.
First I stand in jockey shorts,
carry urine in a paper cup,
as all us guys joke around
about not spilling a drop,
then a stern-faced soldier
orders me to look at the screen
and tell him what I see.
When I say nothing he snaps
"Speak up! Cat got your tongue?
God damn it, tell me what you see."
"I'm waiting," my near-sighted
reply, "for the machine to focus."

An Inside Job

For three summers I sell
bait, boats, fishing permits
at Evans Lake to those
lunatics who show up
before dawn to hook their fill
of perch, bass, and bluegills.
An old Black man likes to gig
for carp along the shore line,
most men want to be out
on the water—fine with me,
I am free to read a good book
by lunch when the fishermen
dock, drive off with their catch.

One morning, I am late
as usual, cars are lined up,
men stand hands on hips
scowling as I unlock
the gate—but the back door
is open, so is the safe:
Someone, during the night,
has robbed the boathouse.
The detective, decked out
in a TV trench coat, asks
a few questions, paces back
and forth, catches my eye.
"Looks like an inside job."
A lie detector would tell.

Headquarters, in Youngstown,
where the usual suspects
are wiseguys implicated
in gangland bombings. I sit
in a third floor room below
a bare bulb—a strap

41

across my chest, fingers
attached, the questioning
begins. Yes or no my options,
I affirm my name, address,
deny I robbed the safe
or know about the theft.
At the end, a dim smile
for my inquisitor, I ask
how I'd done. "Not very good,
Bill." And he shows me
the zig-zagging printout
proclaiming my guilt.

"Either you did this or you
know who did" I am told.
"We have your address.
You'll be hearing from us."
For weeks I rarely slept.
The crime remains unsolved.
All these years I ponder
why my doorbell never rang.
The city cops are swamped,
or snug in the mob's pocket,
no bombers stand trial.

Why did I fail the test?
When Keats saw a sparrow
pecking the gravel he became
that bird, felt its satisfaction.
A crowbar for the door,
sensitive fingers cracked
the safe, loot crammed in a bag,
I made a clean getaway.
In my defense I plead poetry.

II

The Cottonmouth in the Outhouse

The Delta

Above Yazoo City a fertile crescent
covers Mississippi's northwestern corner.
Here for eons floodwaters leave a rich
alluvial soil yielding crop after crop
of cotton. When I drive across the Delta
I think how easy it is to believe
the world is flat and ends at the levee.
For monotonous miles a narrow road,
shimmering in the heat like a mirage
of distant water, fades in front of me
as cotton fields blur by on both sides.

An occasional weatherboard shack,
tin roof flashing in the sun, breaks
this deep green sea of sameness.
A haze of dust hangs over the land,
sticks in the throat, coats my skin
the same rusty brown as the earth.
Scattered far back among the rows,
my sweat-stung eyes glimpse another part
of the picture—heads protected by caps,
hats, handkerchiefs from the relentless sun,
Black sharecroppers drag white sacks.

Then I realize that all those dark
cruddy balls scattered by the roadside,
like thousands of discarded Kleenex,
are old puffs and snarls of cotton too.

The Mansion

for William Faulkner

Walk down a half-mile lane,
an arching tunnel of trees,
old moss-bearded cypress.
Suddenly the gaunt, gutted
soot-blackened shell
of the great house itself
rises in a grove of white oaks.
Wisteria clings in tatters
from the rotted wooden trellis.
Remnants of bougainvillea
lean against a lengthy veranda
once arrayed with wicker chairs.
Here a white man sat napping,
his son leaned against a pillar
drinking from a decanter,
as a Black man mowed the lawn.

Out in the fields stooped slaves
bent over picking the rows,
dragging their long cotton sacks
through the dust behind them,
unmindful of the red-eyed driver
flicking his whip in the air
and the stern overseer sitting up
straight on his sweating horse.

White paint flecks off
the rotting portico, plaster
scales from exterior walls.
The collapsed staircase
with its broken bannister
clutters the barren hall
once lined with stamped leather

imported from Spain. Hand-
hooked rugs once covered
the cypress floors. There was
French walnut furniture,
oil portraits of ancestors.

Behind the summer kitchen,
the scuppernong arbor
and the skeletal chimneys
of broken-backed outbuildings—
fallen stables, gin house,
blacksmith shop, slave quarters.
The formal gardens where ladies
once walked in frail brocades,
twirling their parasols,
are all overgrown, the stone
well is choked with weeds.

A cool breeze through crisp leaves
whispers to you as you depart
the sonorous defeated names
of gone old ghost times.

The Town

Miles away you see a water tower
and bean elevator above the steeples,
then Bobby's Welding Service—WE BUY
WRECKED BURNED JUNKED CARS—
Howard's Peppermint Lounge, Bel Air Court,
the Cherokee Motel, Bubba's Bar-B-Q,
Alfonso's Steakhouse with the plaster steer
on the roof. In the square the stopped clock
at the courthouse, a cast-iron Johnny Reb
on his cement pillar, shirt-sleeved merchants
in doorways, grainy wood-carved faces
of country people in overalls, pursed lips
and pinched faces of local biddies, and always
tragic faces of Black folk, lean men slouching
in straw hats, fat women in red calico,
ragtag and bobtail children with sullen eyes.
Good Old Boys in work shirts, blue jeans,
boots, CAT diesel visored hats stare
with tense muscles and inchoate hate
out of dull gunmetal-blue eyes at sidewalks
steaming in shimmering heat. When one
speaks they all laugh. The squat sheriff
leans on his white machine, blinking old,
cold, yellow-green lion eyes against the glare,
not a clot of recollection of the night he
clubbed a screaming black man down
on the courthouse lawn. The whole town
listened—and re-elected him.

The Shack

The pickers are long gone,
only a few men have jobs.
Cotton choppers replaced by
crop-dusting planes spraying
weed-killing poison. Green
machines resembling gigantic
grasshoppers, bloated bins
for bellies, gobble cotton,
leaving only the ends of rows
for the last of the pickers.

The planter says it's decent
to give tenants a "furnish"
to last through winter,
doesn't see it as a link in
a brutal chain of bondage.
To clear land to seed
for soybeans and cotton
he only lets them plant
a two-row truck patch
by the shack's doorstep,
makes them relocate
the outhouse closer.

The walls have holes
cardboard can't cover,
window frames hold
no glass or screens,
the ground is visible
through floorboards,
the roof leaks come rain
or snow, wind howls
night and day. To stay
warm they stoke the stove
so hot everyone sweats.

It cools down so fast
the young all catch colds,
the old sicken and die.

The kids sleep three or more
in a bed, the table lacks chairs
so they eat from tin plates
on the floor. For drinking
and washing they collect
rainwater in a rusty pail.
At both lunch and dinner
pinto beans and cornbread,
maybe a jar of Kool-Aid,
one child has "sweet blood,"
another intestinal worms,
a doctor might see them
once a year, a dentist never,
only come Christmas time
will they taste fresh fruit.

A Lynching in Mississippi

15 December 1923

We sit in shade on the back patio,
sip lemonade, talk of lynchings
in the Delta. Joe Pullen's name comes up.
A tenant dispute with his landowner,
W. T. Sanders, over who owes whom what.
Joe uses money he believes he is due
to fix his house, buy food for his family.

Sanders rides out to Pullen's place
along with A. L. Manning, a family
now known for star quarterbacks.
Joe meets them, right hand in pocket,
on the front porch. Sanders demands
fifty dollars; Joe pulls out a pistol,
shoots him in the heart.

Some say Sanders had a gun, too,
may have fired first. Manning races
into Drew, soon a sheriff's posse
of a hundred men is in hot pursuit
of Joe, hiding deep in a bayou.
When hounds sniff out his lair
he opens fire with deadly effect.

Three men drop on the spot, others
badly wounded. Manning, hit in the face,
dies the next day. Joe takes his stand
inside a hollow stump half-sunken
in a ditch. To burn him out the mob
pours gallons of gasoline, lights a match,
a machine gun mows him down.

Still alive, he is tied by his ankles,
dragged through the dusty streets of Drew
to cheers, honking horns, a gruesome
procession. His body left by the road,
a severed ear, preserved in alcohol,
on display in a storefront window
for a long, long time.

Fannie Lou Hamer, a girl in Ruleville,
recalls Joe as a local hero.
He had killed him some white men.
Drew imposes a curfew—any Blacks
seen after sundown are fair game.
Landlords become more circumspect
"settling up" debts with sharecroppers.

The Hough Riots

July 1966
Some call it blight. I call it tragedy.
—Carl Stokes, mayor of Cleveland 1967-1971

That summer I am a graduate student
at Western Reserve University
teaching bonehead English at Fenn College
as it morphs into Cleveland State.
First day I tell my class the authors
we will read specialize in
depicting human suffering and pain.
"Write a paragraph," I tell them,
"on a book that changed your life."
Within minutes a gaunt figure strides up,
slaps a page on my desk, and leaves,
slamming the door. Here is what he wrote:
"I denounce you and your decadent books.
The Fountainhead by Ayn Rand taught me
that human suffering is an illusion.
Each man is the captain of his soul,
success comes to the strong of will,
those who fall behind are to blame
for their failures and so-called pain.
You shall not see my face in class again."
My debut as a college teacher
is off to a splendid start.

I live near University Circle
by Murray Hill, known as Little Italy.
My route downtown on Euclid
to Fenn Tower, the campus skyscraper,
runs along the edge of Hough,
a middle-class neighborhood turned
by white flight into a Black slum.
The trouble starts in a café at
79th Street and Hough Avenue.

The dispute is about a glass of water
and a bottle of wine. Rumors fly
that the owner insulted a customer.
A crowd gathers, throws rocks,
tries to burn the building. Firefighters
on the scene are shot at, forced
to retreat.The riot spreads across
the business strip of Hough, windows
broken, stores looted and torched.
Police use tear gas to disperse the mob,
are fired upon from nearby rooftops.

Next night people toss Molotov cocktails,
tip over and burn police cruisers.
In response all of Hough is sealed off,
a helicopter hunts arsonists and snipers.
A fortuitous thunderstorm puts a damper
on the volatile situation, next morning
the National Guard arrives in force.

Driving down Euclid on my way to teach
my class, an armed jeep on each corner,
.30 caliber machine gun mounted
on a platform in back. Young guardsmen
in combat gear, helmets, fixed bayonets,
check my car for weapons then
wave me on. From a window
in my classroom high up in Fenn Tower,
I can see the extent of the damage.
Block after block Hough is smoldering,
dark smoke billows up, sporadic shots
sound amid the cries of sirens.
The riots last three more days.

For years the official story blames
Black Nationalists, Communist subversives.
If any radicals on the scene sniped
at firemen from rooftops none are caught.
Two cops who infiltrate the movement
find no evidence to convict—the cause
rooted in racism, poverty, years of neglect.
Four Blacks die—one gunned down by punks
from Murray Hill in a car—fifty people injured,
far worse inner-city riots take place
in the sixties. What happens at Hough
I witness from a safe-enough distance.
The suffering and pain are not mine.

The Village Scene

for John Strausbagh

1

I wear a black turtleneck, black slacks,
Ginsbergesque horn-rimmed glasses
give an owlish look—a wannabe poet,
existentialist and part-time beatnik,
a beret flopping on my head,
bongo drum protruding at my hip
like some tumorous growth,
and sporting a moth-eaten
Maynard G. Krebs sweatshirt
hacked off at the elbows,
I am just one more jive hepcat,
a finger-popping Daddy-O digging
the scene. In high school I like
the smooth clean sound of
the Kingston Trio but I come
to the village to hear the raw
raspy songs of Dave Van Ronk,
the more rough and gravelly
the more authentic, and I can't
resist the soaring heavenly notes
of Joan Baez. Back then women
sang like angels, men like ex-cons
who work on the docks.

2

John Lindsay, the Go-Go mayor,
an upper-crust Ivy League progressive,
promises a brighter future
but can't pay the city's workers
decent wages. Garbage piled
to eye level on the sidewalks,
the stench is unspeakable,

racial tensions at the breaking point,
parts of the Bronx bear an eerie
resemblance to bombed-out Berlin.
Washington Square, one more
needle park, junkies sprawl on stone
benches once home to chess players,
as Black guys in Afros and dashikis
shout power to the people then offer
to sell cheap whatever it is you need.
I glimpse an addict in a doorway
shoot dope in his scrotum. Pigeons,
heads bobbing, the only sanity
in sight, snap up bread crumps
proffered by a few brave old timers.

3
Fourteenth Street ends at the
Gansevoort Market where butchers
in bloody aprons slaughter beef,
pack great red slabs in trucks all day,
while by night the gay crowd
amble down the cobblestones
cruising for an anonymous quickie,
maybe an orgy, they call it
"taking the express," as opposed
to the local. Others favor "tearooms,"
men's johns in subway stations,
like the one on Christopher street
near Sheridan Square. In this era
the Macho Man look is in:
tight jeans, white T-shirts,
boots and leather jackets.

The color of the bandana
in the back pocket signals
sexual tastes: black for S&M,
green if you charge a fee.
Much of the action takes place
in the back of those same trucks,
rear flap left open to the air,
that haul meat by day.

Dylan

A sharp-featured skinny
angel with a frizzy
halo of reddish-brown
curly hair tousled like
a fright wig, brambled
in tangles and knotted
by the wind—wearing a
snap-brimmed corduroy
Huck Finn cap, blue jeans,
brown jacket, his head bent
to the lost ghost wail
of his sad harmonica,
an acoustic guitar strapped
over his shoulder, scraps
of songs crumpled up
in his pockets—a scruffy
runt defiantly slinging
street words into poem/songs
putdowns and prophecies—
exalted on high-heeled
hand-tooled battered
desert boots, this sunken-
eyed seer back from
a badlands death trip
looks into the dark
like a night hawk
with grim wit he whines
his rhymed visions—
the poetry of apocalypse.

Woodstock

15-17 August 1969

A cow pasture on White Lake
by the Catskill town of Bethel.
The promoters plan
for 50,000, get 400,000,
fees impossible to collect,
thus two million is lost.
Then rains come, farm
devolves to swamp. Despite
a lack of food, water, toilets,
everybody behaves well:
we skinny dip, pop pills
(I am handed a blue one,
"Here. Eat some sunshine"),
pass fragrant peace pipes,
dance to whatever groovy
tunes or raucous vibes shake
loud speakers, rock the stage.
At Woodstock a mob of flute-
tooting pot-smoking flower people
wallowing in a field of black mud
prove we can get along—with
a little help from our friends—
if we're sufficiently stoned.

Tripping

We keep the windows up
and the air conditioner on
smoke joint after joint,
hours become days, time
slips out of sync as we
make our merry way across
the Great Plains. We've read
On the Road, our destination
California. Tom thumps
and strums a broken-
stringed guitar, wails tunes
about how United Fruit abuses
banana pickers. Folk songs,
you see, make a statement,
we gather in the name
of something. We roll
our own, do it in the road,
believe that if everyone
will light just one little
draft card what a peaceful
world this will be.

              The times
are a-changing, ours is
a ragtag army of activists.
Our revolution not waged
by proletariat in factories
or peasants out in the fields,
but students in dormitories.
Politics isn't what you
argue for but what you *do.*
The best way to stop a war
is not to fight in it.

Gutsy is good, if your body
isn't on the line you have
no moral stance. We
oppose the Vietnam war
to avoid dying there, when
four students at Kent State
are killed, protests stop
because we fear dying *here*.
What can you expect of troops
commanded by Sgt. Pepper?

The Cottonmouth in the Outhouse

for James Agee and Walker Evans

1
We take a fast, four-wheeled roll
out of the bluegrass country,
heading southeast on the freeway
for the Cumberland Mountains.

Past fenced-off federal land,
a green, groomed tree farm,
sandy hills, fallow fields,
and broken stalks of corn,

we exit onto a rutted road
and rattle-ass along a humpbacked, corkscrew country lane
with raw, red, eroding shoulders.

We pass a cow haunch-high
in a scum-covered pond
who thinks this is a good place.
We see torn dogs, dead tires.

We pass a two-pump gas station
and a one-room general store.
Out front squatting men
sift dirt, pass the whiskey.

The first shack we see
is a crucified pine
box of a house, bone-bare,
of warped, weathered wood.

And the first woman we see
has a thin, sagging face,
wears a loose, shapeless dress,
resents being looked at.

Her undernourished children
have crusty, cut, dew-poisoned feet.
They wear T-shirts and ride bicycles
just like they had a future.

2
All the old cars in America
know when their time has come.
At night they crawl deep
into the mountains of Kentucky
and roll over on their backs
in front of a clapboard shack,
whose sprained and sagging wood
is tender with rottenness,
whose porch somehow supports
a lidless washer, a busted rocker,
and die there, spewing parts
all the way down to the creek.
These old, outdated notions
suffer crude amputations
and endure the thrown rocks
that spiderweb their windshields.
Stripped of their wheels,
they are set up on cement blocks
where high and frowsy weeds
tickle their chassis
and gardens of springs
sprout in their back seats
as sun-blistered paint
flakes off from side panels
where rust burns in fine particles
that sift into the earth.

3

I've never seen such bleak
bitter beauty, nor a mouth
so hungry, her upper lip
is feeding on her lower,
sucking it partially
into her mouth, her black hair
is draped in clammy ranks
across her head, her eyes
have seen so much of death
and denial that they are frozen
into one mute neutral stare
for all occasions. The wind-
textured unpainted boards
behind her head are part
of her and where she lives.
Her dress is of light cotton
covered with a thousand dots.
It all composes into hard
flat surfaces in blacks
and whites, in horizontal
agonies, nailed with iron.

4

The hard agate marbles
that are his eyes
have seen better days—
but not by much.
The hairs on his head
and on his face
have always gone
their own way—
and he lets them.

The stubble on his chin
runs halfway
down his neck
where a torn T-shirt
opens in a deep
V at the throat.
He is soaked with sweat
at his armpits
and a hot square
on his chest marks
the shape of his overalls.
He's always gone
his own way, though
there aren't that many
ways to go, that's
one thing he learned
early. He wears
an old hat perforated
by shotgun pellets.
It keeps the sun
out of his eyes
while letting the air
cool his head.
He stands hands on hips
at the edge of the porch,
a rigidly proud man
with wary appraising eyes.
As we pass by, his
hound at his feet, he
spits in the dust.

5

This daughter will be a farmer's wife
all her life. She'll bend for days
on end over a small weedy garden,
but she'll never grow nor ever see
two finer flowers than her blue-
green wide and open eyes are.

The great sweeping circle
of her matted straw sun hat
is one of the last extravagant gestures
she will ever know. Her lips this day
are parted as if in anticipation
of possible laughter. Her patterned dress

is starchy clean and the few visible
strands of her just-cut hair are
frail gold on her forehead. There are
already a few faint lines around
her eyes, but they recede in favor
of the freckles on her nose.

Southern Belle

At fifteen she thinks
a girl can't get pregnant
until eighteen, the boy works
at a possum rendering plant,
a potato chip factory, then
a petro-chemical complex
before they split but she
lands on her feet, not bad
for a baton-twirling majorette,
her cartwheels notorious
for a flash of silk panties.
A degree from the local
beauticians college, she
opens her own shop,
marries up, porticoed home
pictured in *Town & Country,*
her hubby, a wealthy lawyer,
loves her honeydew drawl.

Something in the tilt
of the mouth hints her lips
savor kissing each other.
On the side she runs a little
life of her own her man
knows nothing of. To keep
in his good graces she sets
the alarm for six, bathes,
fixes her hair, sneaks back
to bed so when he wakes
she'll look perfect. Once
she takes his Jag, picks up
a hitchhiker, disappears
on a honky-tonk spree.

Sunk in the tub pondering
suicide, razor in hand she
notes hairy legs, cuts a shin,
in a rush to stop the blood
forgets her plan. In time
it comes to pass she slips
off with a roustabout guy,
bouncing dice in windshield,
plastic Jesus on the dash.

Honky-Tonk

Grappling the serpent
on a Saturday night
shape of a scrawny
dishwater blond
sad hound-dog face
her smile a grimace
as if in gastric distress
clinging to a steel pole
to render her artistries
her ribald repartee for
crinkled bills stuffed
in sequined panties.

Cinder-block roadhouse
knee-deep in weeds
neon sign bubbling in
window was what
passed in these parts
for a mead hall. Band
drowned out by popped
tops of beer cans, hoots
and hollers of razorback
rowdies, a caterwauling
crew stomping hoedown
on a scarred wooden floor
raising dust and hell
to celebrate one more
dusk-to-dawn saturnalia.

Nightwatch

Lexington, Kentucky, 1971

Blackbirds clot
at the top of the tree
bare beneath a pale moon
that breaks in half
and swims through
a dark sea of clouds.
Have I mentioned
a strong night wind
whistling down
desolate streets?
The cries of those birds
mastering the air?
How we looked up,
standing on Cheapside,
beside the ominous Gothic
stone courthouse
and found ourselves lost
in a de Chirico landscape.
under an El Greco sky,
lonely and modern?

Assassinating Nixon

17 March 1971

My chance comes at the burial
of Whitney Young, Lexington's
native son, head of the Urban League
who sometimes supported the president.
That's why Nixon came, and I go
to check out Tricky Dick. Although
it's a hot day I notice several tall men
in raincoats whispering to their lapels
as they sidle closer to me.

In those carnivalesque days I am
a college professor who dresses
as a hippie—beaded headband,
hair down to my shoulders,
a Fu Manchu mustache, a puffy-
sleeved shirt of many colors—
signifying, I later realize, that I
must be a suspect character.
I am positioned a few feet away
when the limos arrive.

Nixon pops out, madly grinning
and waving his arms in the air
as if the pit-pat of applause
he receives equaled an ovation.
What strikes me most is his outsized head, how thickly his makeup
is layered on. He looks unreal,
a manikin, and yes if I had a pistol
I could easily shoot him.

It seems someone *has* threatened
Nixon's life. That's why
secret servicemen comprise half
the crowd, why they pinpoint me
as a person of interest. When his
family realizes Young's resting place
is in a segregated part of the cemetery
they rebury him in New York.

Guru Maharaj Ji

Amherst, 7 July 1974

That evening I go to see Guru Maharaj Ji,
Perfect Master and Lord of the Universe.
Women in white with white cloths devoutly
dust his sacred throne inside a towering
Plexiglas helmet seemingly designed for
gigantic astronauts to walk on the moon.
The at-one-with-the-all-be-here-now crowd
in their flower-decaled Beetle vans
trailing clouds of marijuana smoke
have been arriving all day. Now in full
tie-dyed hippie regalia they pack
a large field. A rock band stokes the scene
with ecstatic renditions of "Soul Vaccination
(Got my Soul Vaccination)" and "Gonna See
My Guru Tonight." Some hours later
a silver limo delivers the guru,
a Krishna-costumed chubby teenager,
and his svelte twenty-something consort—
the brains behind the operation, she
enthuses about the miraculous powers
of Maharaj Ji to bring the world peace.
When his turn comes, "There are no words
to say," he says. "Everything is beautiful,"
and his devotees—arms on high, faces
aglow to the star-scattered sky—
absorb his message as blesséd manna.

Americana

She is a Hopi,
he a Pequot, both
adopted by white
parents who live
in Boston. They have
degrees from MIT,
are expecting,
plan to return to
the Hopi reservation
so that their child
can grow up Indian.
The Hopi, however,
are very traditional.
They don't accept
mixed marriages.
Yet he is sure
his high-tech skills
will prove useful
and win acceptance.
"I'll tell them what I
bring to the table,"
he keeps repeating,
as if convincing us
is the same as
convincing them.

Key West

A cat named Archibald
Macleish is asleep
in the master bedroom,
the headboard taken
from an ornate Spanish
gate. "He knows
the rules," the girl says.
"No cats in the house,
but after his picture
was in our brochure he
won't listen to reason."

Pauline takes down
the essential ceiling fans
and replaces them with
her collection of
chandeliers, causing
the guides every summer
to curse her memory.

"This house is the second
highest ground in Key West,"
the guide says. "Sixteen feet
above sea level." When I
chuckle he glances at me
and asks, "Do you feel giddy?"

Louis' Basque Corner

for Frank and Holly Bergon

If you're bored by Reno's casinos,
those ersatz palaces of glitz,
and hunger for sturdy food
Louis' Basque Corner is the place.
The old railway towns of Nevada
had small hotels by their stations
where Basque sheepherders
from Spain and France found
the basic comforts of home.

After summering in the mountains
and deserts with their flocks,
in the winter they sought bed
and board at a Basque hotel.
Hearty fare, family style
on long communal wooden tables
covered by well-worn oilskin,
Louis' restaurant remains faithful
to this culinary ritual.

Start with a Picon Punch:
in an ice-packed glass pour
Amer Picon, a bittersweet orange-
flavored liquor from Marseilles,
add a dash of grenadine, a splash
of soda, a flourish of brandy,
a rim-twist of lemon. Alumni
of this potent aperitif caution:
one, two, three, floor.

Sharing a meal turns strangers into
accomplices, we're all elbow-to-elbow
as waiters arrive with "the set-up,"

vegetable soup, a house salad
featuring heirloom tomatoes,
bowls of slow-cooked white beans,
pungent bread, crisp fries fluffy on
the inside, sprinkled with garlic bits,
heaping platters of roast chicken.

Topping the fulsome prelude
a selection of savory entrées:
mountain oysters in season,
sweetbreads in two styles—sautéed
in garlic and onions or soaked
in a red-wine mushroom sauce—
beef tongue or oxtail stew,
juicy lamb chops or lamb shank,
prime rib, steak to your taste.

This Basque bacchanal is abetted by
carafes of cabernet, tall mugs of beer,
plates are passed, toasts proffered,
good talk flows and feelings glow.
Don't forget dessert: ice cream,
a tangy variety of cheeses,
fresh fruit, and strong coffee.
Give thanks for this ample feast—
and for stopping at two Picons.

Prospecting

for A. R. Ammons

Coming to traffic lights,
an orange restaurant,
an alley edged
with parking meters,
I leave my car nosed against
the cement curb.
Dazzled by the hot sun
and my loneliness
like a politician I go
out and shake
hands with the postman,
and running up the gray street
tug the neon sign
up and over into light,
on a hill of shops
call out my purchases
telling each salesman
exactly what I want.
At dusk someone
pulls on a handle
turning on the street lights.
At dawn returning, flat
out of cash, my loneliness
wakes me up, we
shower and shave,
refreshed for a new day.

The Tornado

1
Heat lightning on the horizon,
leaves shiver, show
their silver undersides.
In the middle distance
a thunderbolt detonates,
rain pelts down in sheets,
rising above the tree line
a hooded head curls
like a cobra. When it
flashes its fangs and strikes
our whole town collapses
into a vacant space
of scattered sticks and bricks.

2
When the sirens sound
we open all the windows
just a crack and head
for the root cellar
to sit out the storm—
but that year the hit
was direct, only
the root cellar left
with us still in it.
Nobody hurt, not
even a scratch.

3

One farmer went out
in the storm to care for
his stock, next morning
we find his body near
the cow barn transfixed
by flying straw blown
by the wind so hard
long yellow needles
were driven deep in
fence posts, tree trunks,
barn siding too.

Hoffa

Hoffa!—a name like a shout.
A working stiff, he'd rather settle
matters with his fists. "Do unto others—
first" was his motto. He has a surly,
truculent grandeur—shoving a grapefruit
into a dame's face á la James Cagney
his opening gambit. A tough guy
straight off the loading docks,
he takes on the Kennedys like
John Henry vs. the steam drill.

Before his birth an Indiana doctor
thinks his mother has a tumor,
hence his ugly nickname as a kid.
When the family moves to Detroit,
at Fisher Body he polishes radiator caps.
For his first strike as a Teamster
the men refuse to load strawberries:
negotiate, they say, or watch
them rot. Back in those days
cops smack you upside the head
just for talking union.

          He tells his locals
his job is to get working men
top dollar, not to throw no picnics.
He wears white socks, snores
at the opera, but doesn't run around
on his wife Josephine; the one time
he dances, his daughter's wedding.
No cussing at home, the union hall
something else, his lips twitch
saying "sonofabitch"—he makes no
idle threats.

A stand-up guy,
he beats rap after rap but never
shoulda bad-mouthed Bobby
or gone to that restaurant
to meet Tony Jack and Tony Pro.
Everybody kept asking where Jimmy
is buried, no one assumes
he's ascended into heaven. Yet
"Hoffa" shouted loud enough
is not an empty sound.

Urban Renewal in Detroit

GM wants land in Detroit
for a central industrial park
to employ six thousand workers—
Poolestown is the target.
Graffiti appears on the walls
of demolished buildings,
"Death to Arsonists, Thieves,
and GM." Proud people
refuse to leave, city services
decline, then disappear,
crime is on the rise.
A SWAT team drives the last
protesting squatters out
of Immaculate Conception,
then it's taken down in days.

To replace Poolestown the city
builds the world's largest
resource recovery plant,
in other words it burns
an inferno's worth of trash
to turn it into energy.
It seemed like a good idea.
The problem is pollutants
pour out of the stacks,
spread carcinogens
across the neighborhood.
The protestors' slogan:
"We all live downwind."
When the plant fails
to show a profit the city
sells it to Philip Morris,
who supposedly promises
to deal with the problem
of smoke causing cancer.

The Corner

for David Simon

Oh Baltimore / Man, it's hard just to live.
                    —Randy Newman

West Baltimore is not one of Dante's
descending circles of Hell,
just block after block of red-brick
flat-roofed rowhouses with puny
adjacent porches gaping at streets
that weave a rectangular maze
from which few escape.

Every morning fiends gather
at the corner where touts
chant brand names—*Killer Bee,*
Lethal Weapon, The Terminator—
for a sample taste of the day
and then spread the word
this shit is the bomb, a blast
that will last, bring back that first
soul-shattering high they crave
to ravish themselves again.

It's a strictly a cash-and-carry
business for the coke-crazed
pulling capers to make the nut.
Copper piping, aluminum siding,
steel fittings from construction sites
sold to Union Iron and melted down.
Or ransacking apartments, lugging off
the loot in black Hefty bags. Whatever
you boost, part of the game.

Each corner an open-air bazaar
for crews with the best package
money can buy (if they can hold
their ground), an oasis drawing
predator and prey—vacant-eyed
fiends wander in like wildebeests
to slack their thirst, jackals, big cats,
vultures primed to feed on
the weak and unwary—while
snatch artists eye touts slinging vials
for a chance to steal their stash.

Stickup boys, lone wolves
with long guns, shakedown
well-heeled dealers or rip
plywood from derelict buildings
in a testosterone rush to raid
shooting galleries, squalid dens
where the far-gone sprawl on floors
littered with pipes or spikes,
a few blackened bottle caps,
some matches, a jar of water,
each fiend seeking the holy grail
in a glassine bag or plastic vial.

Like a barrel of blue crabs
anyone trying to climb out is
dragged back down. If you get
jacked by cops for conspiracy
with intent to distribute, a stint
at Hagerstown, a chance to give
tired veins a rest. *Wine is fine,
so is dope, yet nothing is finer
than a toke of that ready rock.*

The message: don't mess with desire.
Once you do your own jail time
the corner will still be there.

Crime Scene

In West Baltimore a man in blue
watches a human body cool.
Blood droplets speak, so do spent
bullets, shell casings, how a body
falls if it fell where it is found.
Tiny fibers yield trace evidence.
A latent print. The first officer
to arrive is supposed to protect
the crime scene instantly starting
to deteriorate, but officer Jenkins
wanders off, uses the john, stops
for coffee and a doughnut on his
way to the hospital, drives home
when his shift is up, while others
contaminate evidence, step
in blood, touch suspicious objects,
filch what strikes their fancy.
A shrewd lawyer counts on cops
to bungle the scene of a crime
enough for reasonable doubt.

When backup squad cars arrive
the cops seek witnesses, ask
what went down. "I ain't seen
nothing, man," a shake of the head,
averted eyes, hands dancing on air,
the usual gestures. The code
of the hood hates a snitch.
This body is found in a bedroom,
no forced entry, no strange fingerprints,
which swiftly narrows the field
to family members and friends.
A Baltimore homicide detective
wastes no time suspecting the butler,
or some criminal mastermind,

here murders are domestic disputes
or drug-related; he studies not why
but how—a steak knife with
a broken blade, stab wounds
to hands and chest, blood splatter
of a struggle——the mean streets
will provide who and motive.

Jury Duty

Three-time loser on a daily basis,
a drunkard, a pill-popper, the thief
smashes a gas station's glass door,
cuts his wrist as he reaches inside
to open it, snatches some cash, runs
to a nearby pharmacy for bandages.
The cops merely follow his drops
of blood, snap on the handcuffs.
Open and shut. Old Home Week
at the local slammer coming soon.

Police in a helicopter spot marijuana
rising above a remote cornfield
in the Catoctins. Frederick County's
finest Keystone Krew crash-land
their craft but still nab suspects.
Four brothers farm the land,
swear innocence on the Bible,
tall pot plants plainly visible
from windows of their shacks.

Since my notes are sequestered,
I can't recall the mangled phrases
of these latter-day Jukes and Kallikaks
whose sexual mingling, shall we say,
beggars belief. I've lived in Kentucky,
know my Appalachian twangs, yet
strain to decipher the garbled mumblings
of this backwoods brood. Someone
needs to turn state's evidence for us
to bring an indictment—two know
their wives are sleeping with a brother,
but nobody dares rat on the clan.

Final case, a twenty-something guy
leads the police on a high-speed chase
down I-270. The cops can't catch him
but trace the car to his sister's house.
A bartender admits he was intoxicated,
denies watching him drive off. A policeman
testifies even through tinted windows
he could see him behind the wheel.
My take: one is witholding evidence,
the other provides too much.

Though no stranger to a few glasses
of wine, speeding at over a hundred-
miles-an-hour down a major highway
is attempted murder in my book.
The defendant, aiming his steely
wolfish gaze at me, is guilty as hell.
Several jurors take pity on
the punk and refuse to convict.

Jurors don't set aside their egos,
see everything through the lens of self.
They'd rather not debate or sort
conflicting testimony. All doubts
are reasonable if they can go home.
Dressed in suit and tie the suspect
looks innocent enough to acquit.
As the sage says: if you want justice,
go to Heaven, here you get the law.

Active Shooter

On guns and grievances

1
In high school halls students
debate which classmate is
most likely to kill them all.
Could be the guy in combat boots
who spits at girls, calls them sluts,
or the jock who grabs his crotch
if anybody sexy walks by.
Perhaps some weird nerd
who laughs out loud for no
good reason. My money is on
the Goth guy dressed in black
with gruesome tattoos crawling
up his neck, a small swastika
on his forehead. He's a good bet
to show up one day in a flack
jacket, an automatic that fires
a hundred rounds in seconds,
a heart bursting with grudges.

Whoever the next shooter
chances are he'll be white,
a loner, quiet, keeps to himself,
secretly enraged, quick-tempered,
seething inside to get even.
He spends lots of time playing
violent video games, gets off
on revenge fantasies drenched
in gore, heads blown off by
high-tech weapons *de rigueur*.
He's like a lot of boys who
would never do what he did.

How can we separate the gamer
from the game? Why must
others pay for his fury
with their lives?

2
A gunman shoots up a Walmart
where Mexicans like to shop,
a workplace to settle scores with
his pushy boss who fired him,
some fellow workers that say
things he doesn't like. The victims
are Jews in a Synagogue, Blacks
at church, classmates at desks,
Mom and Dad who wouldn't
let him have a pickup truck.
The rare Black shooter might
ambush cops, if an Islamic fanatic,
his target a local bar, a party,
or the truly perverse might turn
a semiautomatic on first-graders
at Sandy Hook Elementary.

Reporters seek sense in
senseless murders, motives
where there are none, no logic,
just a sudden notion to kill.
Crazy acts in a crazy world
we refuse to admit is our own;
we choose to believe people
who commit the worst crimes—
irredeemable, unforgiveable—

have reasons. Or we blame
mental illness. The truth
is simple: a white guy,
a grievance, a gun that fires
too many bullets too fast.

Tay Old Guy

A story of our times

Clara and Kyle meet and bond
at the Maryland Renaissance Festival,
share a fascination with witchcraft,
vampires, the occult. They enter
a fantasy realm, The Underworld,
she is a Priestess of High Chaos,
he a sword-wielding Assassin pledged
to do her bidding: the problem is O. G.,
or Old Guy, her name for her father.
He disapproves of her Goth look,
heavy metal music, Martens shoes,
she swears he pulls her hair, poisons
her pork chops, better if he's out
of the picture. She is a damsel
in distress, Kyle, a knight who vows
to do the noble thing and "tay" Old Guy.
Kyle hears voices tell him this
is a just cause. He drives at night
to Clara's home in Loudoun County
while she stays at James Madison.
When her father opens the door,
Kyle slashes, stabs, and hacks
him with a sword some thirty times,
cuts an X in the back of his neck.
"What did I ever do to you?"
he pleads before he dies. Clara
claims at the trial that her father
abused her; Kyle that fire-breathing
dragons lived during the reign
of King Arthur. He is bipolar,
schizophrenic, institutionalized
seven times. For Clara, this is
her first and last life sentence.

The Sacrament

At the sign of the candy cane
men come to be made clean
on a regular basis. The barber
drapes a cloak on the shoulders,
and, electric razor in hand, unruly
hair falls to the floor as he gives
voice to the sacrament, lends
an attentive ear, as do others
waiting their turn in chairs,
to profane tales of manly folly,
the baffling behavior of women,
and the fucking unbelievable
incompetence of politicians.
These manifold overt and
covert sins are not shrived
but celebrated, as spicy
anecdotes inspire others
to share in the commentary.
The sibilance of the shears
softly severing the last strays,
the warm lather on the back
of the neck, the nape-tingling
scrape of the blade—so precise
and refreshing—the ultimate
application of holy ointments,
and communion, not with God
but mortal men, is complete.

The Ron Reagan Story

A small-minded small-town boy
with big dreams of talking his way
to the top. As a life guard
he rescues seventy-five souls,
he says, from the Rock River,
a radio announcer he describes
towering home runs, slick
double plays he never saw.
At his best as an actor he asks,
"Where's the rest of me?"
At his worst he is upstaged
by chimps. Silent Cal is
smiling Ron's political ideal,
after a Hollywood flirtation
with the Left, dismantling
the New Deal and Great Society
(as well as the Evil Empire)
is his life's work. He thinks
the simple truth can be made
simpler, the Great Communicator
speaks exclusively in clichés—
easy consolations, great expectations—
and steers clear of deep waters
and seas uncharted. He sits back
in his swivel chair as fat
cats grow fatter and the under-
class goes under. He rides
to power on a wink and a grin,
and whatever he wins is for
the Gipper. At the end,
he doesn't know what he knew
and when he forgot it. In death
his life morphs into the myth
of a kind grandfatherly lion
who could do no wrong.

Fascist Kitsch

6 January 2021

Each insurrection has its aesthetics.
Trump's cult, in a deep state of delusion,
storms the Capitol to stop the theft of
an election Biden won by seven million.
They come in outlandish costumes,
in combat camouflage tactical gear
as if on a Special Ops Mission,
others cosplaying characters of choice:
Vikings, Goth invaders, Good Old Boys
primed for a plastered tailgate party.
Whatever the outfit, all are armed
with iPhones to livestream selfies
to co-conspirators across the country.

This is the politics of spectacle,
mad mayhem as performance theater,
acting out a video game where real
blood is shed. Smugly gleeful faces
show how it feels to trash a world
they do not understand. Fantasies
can be dangerous, kitsch can kill,
Trump has whipped his fascist thugs
into a red-hatted rage that ignores
the forces wrecking their lives.
In the name of "freedom" they
stab a dagger into our democracy,
bring lasting harm and shame.

The Christmas Carol War

for James Nolan

One Christmas season in the burbs
two houses, alike in status, vie
to see who can put up the most
outlandishly garish display
of decorations. Waterfalls
of colored lights, frantically blinking,
cascade down from each roof,
while in a strident crescendo
from each bedecked porch blare
dueling versions of "Silent Night"
and "Hark! The Herald Angels Sing."

When lo, under the influence
of laced eggnogs, Jack Stockbroker
aims a pistol at his neighbor's house
across the cul-de-sac, blasting
Santa out of his sleigh atop
the carport and tumbling reindeer
along the driveway. Via shotgun
Phil Pharmacist retaliates,
reducing to smithereens Jack's
life-size crèche and scattering
in plastic pieces Mary, Joseph,
Magi, and assorted sheep
over the grass, into the street.

The baby Jesus is never found.

III

Intimations

Skeleton in the Woods

The moose has no predators.
In its mature strength fearing
neither man nor beast it strides
brazenly down a small town's
main street or halts traffic on
the highway. Even wolves are
wary of its rack of wide-
spread antlers. In Yellowstone
I walk into the woods
beyond a beware of bears sign,
in a sunlit clearing I pause
before a strange sight: Centered
in a circular carpet of dark fur
a gleaming white, perfectly
articulated skeleton of a moose.
As silent and serene as a shrine,
the site still conjures an unsettling
vision of violence, the dead metaphor
"the fur flew" comes to life—picture
the feeding frenzy that could cause
those tufts to float in the air,
fall to earth symmetrically.
Yet within that dark ominous circle
the white ribcage of the moose,
weakened by old age, outlines
the arched framework of a chapel,
a sanctuary to life and death.

Swift Creek

Stepping softly on hardwood duff,
spongy death beneath tall trees,
white moths flutter up from the forest floor
as I wind my way through black oak,
mountain laurel, and umbrella
magnolia in flower all around me.
By the stone bridge where water
falls, I cool my eyes beside the rock-
strewn rapid-running stream.
In the shade of the cottonwoods
I see how sunlight reflects off
the surface, sending rippling patterns
across the bottoms of the leaves.

I watch the water purl over rimrock,
frothing in riffles below the falls.
Here the creek forms a deep pool
where fish backs flash in the sun-
flecked stream. Further down
the water churns into the sandstone
narrows, cutting random outcroppings,
exposing fossils in the shale ledges,
as the current carves and smooths
a crooked path down the gorge
to the green valley.

The Nightingale's Song

When we say birds
find their way by instinct,
what we're saying
is we don't know how
birds find their way.
Nightingales never sing
until they hear another
nightingale singing,
but when they do sing
they know the score
from start to finish,
no beginner's errors.
How can that be?
we ask, answer:
it simply is.

Gator

Mist hangs over the river,
a ghostly aura. Cypress trees
squat in the muck, pink knees
protrude from tan waters, Spanish moss
and old man's beard fringe branches
outstretched as if in lamentation.
Beware of cottonmouths hidden
in the maidenhair along the bank
and alligators basking in the sun
on the muddy shore or sunk in ooze
to their eyeballs. Mouths open to let
hot rays dry their teeth, they seem
dead to the world, yet how quickly
they can slither into the water
and speed to the place where gar
are feeding or a fawn has fallen.
I respect a gator's alert eye,
its talent to catch the least scent
of blood. At a glance I can spot
their lairs along the shore, before
diving into a swimming pool
I inspect the bottom, a glimpse
of a dark retread by the highway
conjures a dire word: "Gator."

The Love Songs of Frogs

In Panama mating calls of túngara frogs
are louder in cities than in rain forests.
The love songs they belt out are longer,
more alluring. They don't croak, croak
like American bullfrogs, their pillow talk
goes beep, beep, beep. At twilight time
horny males seek a mud puddle of choice,
inflating their outsized vocal sacs
to serenade the ladies within sound
of their melodies. Urban frogs, it seems,
jazz up their numbers with staccato chucks
tacked at the end of their plaintive whines.
Tapes of urban tunes are irresistible,
prompting females to hop to the speaker;
whether city gals or country gals,
that syncopated crooning rings
their bell. In the forest male frogs
cool their repertoire—strident chucks
attract bats, snakes, other predators.
Thus it comes to pass that those
brown-skinned inch-long urban dudes
who switch the beat, hit the high notes,
know the score on how to score.

The Courtship of Scorpions

is fraught with danger.
A female primed to mate
emits a perfume, tiny
hypersensitive hairs
on a male's four pairs
of legs bristle, he begins
to judder or shake, sending
randy virbrations, as one
of her eight eyes winks
they quickly *hook up*—
front pincers to pincers
held on high, head
to head, they waltz
forward and back,
taking turns who leads,
who follows. Curled
tails, tipped with a highly
lethal toxin, add the spice
of death to their dance.

To kiss they nibble
mandibles, aroused
he deposits a small packet
of sperm on the ground,
promenades his partner
precisely to the spot
where she must sit down
to complete the deed.
Should he fail this agile
test of strength, she might
inject a fatal sting and eat
him for lunch. If, however,

all goes well, he'll split
the scene and in eighteen
months she'll deliver a large
batch of babies that nestle
on her back until ready
to live out the same cycle
scopions have lived for
one hundred million years.

The World at Low Tide

for Rachel Carson

"She did her homework, she minded her English,
and she cared."
$\qquad$ —David Brown

High above spruce trees
the rosy breast of a soaring gull
catches the glory of the risen sun.
Seabirds skim over tide flats
waiting to feed on what waves
bring in and leave behind.

Line after line of white caps
charge toward the shore,
stumble and are cut down
in sight of the beach, fall
sprawling on the sand.
Then in a froth of confusion
they salaam back to sea
leaving spent shells, debris.

Call it slack tide, ebb tide,
low tide, neap tide,
in this time and place
we see and smell what
the water has left for us.
How far did it come to reach
this shore? Might be continents
or merely local stuff that drifted out
and now comes back.

This stretch of sand is a zone
of transition where sea and land
meet and mingle. This is where
a few fish first dreamed of feet,
whales opted for the deep blue.

We all must adapt and evolve
or stand pat and die. If we don't
protect our planet it will cease
to protect us. In time the surf
will grind these rocks lining
this shore into sand and you
and I will have gone the way
of all mortality.

Dock of the Bay

How to describe this scene—
old scow capsized in black mud,
rot-eaten tub stranded in marshland,
fishing smack sunk to the gunnels in muck,
decayed dinghy belly-up in brackish water,
paint-blistered boat aground in green sludge—
whichever way I say it the stench
of dead fish, the reek of wet weeds,
permeate the tide flats, smothering
the fresh salt smell of the sea.

When the water rises a dark hull
lists slightly, a half-hearted lament for
the incoming surge it will never ride again.
I sit on the dry splintered timbers of the dock,
sluggish waves lipping the pilings,
a gull trolls the air for insects,
skims the breakers, struts on the beach,
where the surf slaps and slides
dragging pebbles along the shore,
scalloping patterns in the sand.

A Life More Abundant

One day she asks her children
home from college for favorite
memories of growing up.
Their response isn't much,
a shared milkshake here,
flat tire there, a trip to Disneyland.
That is my life, she thinks,
everything I do or care about
dishwater down the drain.
She doesn't want to be a housewife
anymore, scrubbing and cleaning,
so she becomes an archeologist
who spends long hours
grubbing in the dark earth,
shaking dirt through a mesh,
sifting dust from dust in quest
of the detritus of the past,
a toothbrush behind her ear
for cleaning up potsherds.
At Meadowcroft on Cross Creek
in western Pennsylvania
under the overhanging arch
of a sandstone cliff, six feet
below surface ground strewn
with beer cans, junkies' needles,
she finds firepit fragments
dating back 16,000 years.

Four Seasons

1
To worship seasonal gods
makes perfect sense to me,
I ask no better grace
than the gift of spring.
One of those April days
that plays a medley of
all weathers—wind, cold,
rain, sleet, and a final
brief flurry of snow,
followed by blue skies
snatches of sunshine,
songbirds whet and sweeten
jingling small silver coins,
singing on the wing.
Overnight leaves uncurl
from buds, a brown world
blossoms in many colors
like a spendthrift painter
splurging a palette of pastels,
a dash of darker hues,
turning the grass green
with envy. Sparrows swirl
by in garrulous clouds,
cheering for the bright side,
chirping sap up maples
that oozes out at a tap.
A breeze blows scented
petals in my face. O uncork
the day, taste the bubbles.

2

Each season states its position
as clearly as sun on stone.
In the hazy dog days of August
hawks make haughty spirals
over the parched land,
pasty hair sticks to the scalp,
sweat stings squinting eyes
as stifling afternoon heat
swamps all thought of thought
for a limp, lackadaisical feeling.
Leaves hang like the tongues
of panting hounds, butterflies
flap by on indolent wings.
Going indoors is worse,
the air conditioner is out,
no shower to cool the skin.
So hot, no drink cold enough
to slack an unrelenting thirst.
Thus we swelter on the porch
and wait for the sun to set,
yet evening takes its sweet time
bringing the slightest comfort
until after midnight a light
breeze provides some relief.

3

When the mind-numbing whine
of leaf blowers assaults your ears,
sets teeth on edge, and a blue haze
of noxious fumes blurs your vision,
stings eyes, seek a backyard shed,
retrieve an old abandoned rake,
test its long thin fingers, spreading
like a lady's fan, of rusty tines,
begin taking desultory swipes
at sunset-colored leaves strewn
across the lawn. No rush in this.
If the wind ruffles a gathering,
lifts and filches a few fugitives,
that's okay. What doesn't get bagged
will molder and rot, living on
as mulch, permeating and enriching
the soil. Comb the green hair
of the grass, the dirt likes
a scratched back, a pungent,
not unpleasant odor will rise
from the earth, a compensation
for childhood memories of the scent
of burning leaves seasoning
the autumn air. Don't probe
dank clumps at the foot of trees
between exposed roots where small
crawly things conceal treasures.
Only scolding squirrels disparage
your ecological ways, fearing nuts
and acorns meticulously stashed
for winter will be discovered.

If at this leisurely pace you tire
easily, why not lie on your back
in a pile of leaves, gaze at clouds
drifting across an azure sky,
watch what flutters down.

4
When the pond is ice-tight
anybody can walk on water,
or skim down a steep hill
on polished slats of wood,
but there is no salvation
in snow which whispers by
telling its white secrets,
snakes across the road
in thin slithering sheets
that cover parked cars,
form humpbacked drifts
before a line of evergreens,
nor in howling blasts of
wind whose frigid knives
cut to the bone. As we look
out windows imprisoned
by icicles at sunlight sparkling
on freshly fallen snow,
trees silvery with hoarfrost,
branches cased in crystal,
there's nothing to do
but pile logs on the fire,
add blankets to the bed,
endure an artic agony of
short cold days, long cold nights,

as we faithfully wait for
the only resurrection
that we're sure is true—
the blessed rebirth of spring.

The Wind

A young cornfield can fall
flat in a windstorm like soldiers
cut down in their prime,
but then the sun comes out
and shines, slowly the stalks
stand again, only to be mown
down in season when rows of
fat ears flaunt their tassels.

The voice of the wind varies,
it can whine or howl then become
soft as a whisper. The invisible
hand of the wind moves what
it touches, look at leaves flutter,
grass bend to its will, waves
kick up, don white caps,
then suddenly subside.

Sometimes the wind sings
a soothing song, other times
it roars like an express train
and tears the house down.
The sound of the wind
is a shifty devil, restless,
always turning itself over
as if in search of something
of value it lost long ago.

Homer Comes Home

"Your cat ran in front
of my truck and got hit,"
the note read. "I put it
in a pizza box near
the back porch. I'm sorry,
but I couldn't stop."

When I lift the lid
one glance at the grey
tail and my eyes glaze
over. Roser will be home
soon and I know she'll be
as heartbroken as me.

I pace the house, look
constantly out windows
for her return from work.
Then, at the back door,
I see our cat Homer
eager to be let in.

What joy! *As the need
is sorest, so the answer
comes soonest*, sings
Lotte Lenya, but then
I see a grey tail
still in the pizza box.

After a door to door
search, I inform a grief-
stricken neighbor it is
her cat that died
while, miraculously,
ours has come home.

Back in the kitchen
I pour myself a large
glass of wine, wait
for Roser to return.
How do I tell her
this sad-happy tale?

Winslow Homer's *The Fog Warning*

A lone fisherman pauses
in his rowing, tilts his head
at ominous fog blowing in
on the dark horizon. Just now
he's heard the mother ship's horn
warning of his danger. The pensive
profile—chin up, calculating how far
he must row for a safe return versus
the approach of an incoming fog
thick enough to leave him blindly lost—
suggests he's confronted this fate
before. What are the odds?
His fists, at canvas center,
firmly grip the oars.

No matter how sturdy the wood
his dory is made of, it is tossed
like a shell, turbulent waves,
cresting whitecaps, lift the prow
skyward with each mighty surge,
plunge back down again as if
to dispatch the boat to the deep.
Two large white halibut in the stern
prove a successful catch, all for naught
should he fail at the heroic task
of rowing to his ship, a small,
ghostly apparition in the distance.
Whether or not he survives
Homer's painting does not show.

Concert Hall

The conductor stands between
a seated orchestra, a seated audience,
she is the woman with the baton
and has the power of life and death
over every instrument, a slight
movement of her hand and they
spring to rousing life or fall silent.
A priest faces the congregation,
not so the orchestra conductor.
She keeps her back to the audience
during the entire performance,
only at the end she turns to them,
they have been quiet, motionless,
pretending to be deaf to rhythms
throbbing through the hall.
Suddenly thunderous applause,
a standing ovation, the only chance
they have to make noise too,
clapping hands as if each secretly
longed to be a cymbal or a drum.

Bread Loaf, 1982: Two Views

1 Politics & Writing
    John Gardner

Everyone should be interested in politics.
Last year we had a shooting war between
two unions over who should harvest
the lettuce, then the government
dumped the lettuce in the ocean.
People are dying while we are trying
to think how to become great writers.
Publishers, readers, the powers that be
don't like writers turning to politics.
It's low class in America to be political.
It's not elegant to be serious.
The New Criticism studied clockwork,
neglected what was being said.
Language in its most sophisticated forms
carries lies, "mankind" is a loaded word.
Our speech has got us by the neck.
Your choice of subject implies
a set of values. To be a great writer
you must feel greatly, you can't write
cheap political shit, yet if you're not
writing politically you're not writing,
but your politics when you begin
a work of fiction ought not to be
the politics you end up with.

2 Ars Poetica
    Howard Nemerov
The middle of the poem is less interesting.
That's why we have an index of first lines.
We ought to have an index of last lines.
Write a good first line and last line,
nobody reads the rest anyway.

Start with simple things, like "mobled queen"
is good. Listen, the line will whisper
what you need to know to continue,
how it wants to be said. The great
advantage of form is that it helps you
to forget what your "message" is.
Editorials by poets are not necessarily
better than editorials by editors.
"A poem should not mean but be."
I learned that by editing a review,
reading lots of poems that didn't mean
anything—but there they were.
Some contemporary poems make you
want to divide poetry into two camps—
and then burn them both. The trouble
with free verse is it doesn't tell you what
to do. Normally you divide the line
according to the grammar and all
the tension is gone. Poetry is
melodiousness, the possibilities
for variation are immense. If you don't
have a line and a stanza there is
nothing to vary. A poem requires
either lilt or balance or drive.
First you must put it together brick

by stupid brick, then make it
sound as if it were effortless.
I told Robert Frost "Spring Pools"
was about growing up, making choices,
settling on a mode of life. He replied,
"I was writing about capillary action."
Poets like to ask big questions,
then go on to other things. "Did she
put on his knowledge with his power?"
Well, did she? Probably not.
I only steal other people's lines
to support my habit.

Postmodern Poetry

The first sentence is
always hard. I'm glad
that's over. Now we can
get down to business.
Allow us to introduce

ourselves. I'm a sentence.
Me too. Watch our progress
down the page. There's no
stopping us. By now you,
our so-called reader,

assuming that you really
exist, want us to get
to the point, but who's
to say what the point is
we reply, don't you

know that everything is
absolutely relative, what
chance do you have if
all of us sentences
gang up on you? This

is *our* narrative, or, if
you prefer, discourse,
"reality" is not real,
words rule, we control
the page, ours is the power.

Hey, wait a minute,
you can't do that to us,
we're speaking here,
where in the world do
you think you're going?

You Numskull

Every paper you turn in
I have to ticket
for drunken driving.
You crash every period,
run over schools of commas
as if they were rabbits.
All your words must be searched
for concealed weapons.

Occasionally an idea escapes
and I have to track it down
through a swamp of syntax
until I finally corner it
in an old ramshackle shack
of a paragraph, but when I
try to take it alive
for questioning
all I find is a body
stabbed to death
with exclamation points!

Campus Wisdom

While we sit in a circle
and sing "Michael knows
the bowling score," she
curls up in the fertile
position and feels asleep.
At the Sermon on the Mount
Jesus preaches the B-attitudes,
he is condomed to death
by the Phallusees, that was
a hyenas crime. I mean
it is a doggy dog world,
don't take anything for granite,
life isn't all fun in games,
it is a mellow drama.
So be a wheel-rounded person,
and don't burn your fingers
before they're crossed.
I learn that in college,
which makes it worth my wild.

Entropy

Everything longs to mingle,
car keys and loose change
play hanky-panky in pockets,
books slide off shelves,
kitchenware and glasses
seemingly secure in cabinets
clatter down and shatter,
pots crack, cookies crumble.
Watch droplets on a leaf
gather, ease together, fall,
or ashes at a cigarette's tip,
the other shoe hits the floor.
Life skews, bends out of shape,
a cant, a slant, awry, akimbo,
out of kilter. There is a sag, slump,
things lurch, topple, collapse,
warp and woof lose alignment,
Humpty Dumpty's off the wall,
lakes desiccate, trees debauch,
tunes jangle, clang discordant.
Even a substance as obdurate
as iron rusts, flakes off in petals.
I'm too tired to finish the list,
it's all dregs down the drain—
each puddle seeks a creek,
wants to slide to the sea.

Intimations

Trapped in time
lost in space
these bones can live
only so long as
the heart beats
lungs breathe
and the warm
flesh is willing
to cling to them.

Hell, Sartre said,
is other people,
which presents
a problem for
this life and that
to come—in the
unlikelihood
that such exists
at whatever
altitude or
temperature.

On Suicide

We held a vote,
my body and I,
if I should die
by my own hand.
My body stood
against the idea,
my mind accepted
the good advice.
For Camus whether
life is worth living
is at the heart
of philosophy—
does our absurd
existence dictate
suicide? My friend
Jim begs to differ:
the key question is
should I get out of
bed in the morning?
Don't die, live,
Camus concludes,
drain the bitter cup
to the dregs, deplete
yourself, remain
unreconciled to
our absurd condition.
Longevity is best,
but not all lives
are equally equal.
Day by day choose,
if you can, quality
over quantity.

Walls

We all serve life sentences,
some receive time off
for good behavior while
the executioner waits.
A few confined to solitary,
others the run of the yard,
the vast majority live
without prison walls,
at least of the cement block,
barbed-wire, iron bars variety.
We are, indeed, free to go
where we wish, provided
we have cash on hand
or a valid credit card,
so why not live it up,
dance the night away,
laze at the beach, scale
mountains, venture
to foreign lands? Yet
in the end everything
comes down to walls.
That's why Bartleby
was obsessed by them,
from those of brick
out his office window
to his final confinement
in the Tombs, staring
at one of massive stone
and telling the lawyer,
"I know where I am."

The Banality of Evil

Crematoria create problems.
The gas is so effective,
you see, all those bodies
pile up on top of one another
and so forth. Corpses
swell and smell, soggy bones
don't burn well. Rest assured
we did many scientific studies
to find the most efficient method
of getting air to circulate freely
inside those heaps of the dead
so that the fire can breathe.

Hiroshima

All clocks stop
at 8:10 a.m.

The dying want
a sip of water,
are too weak
to swallow it.

First nosebleed,
then skin spots.
Touch the hair
it falls out,
touch the skin
it comes off.

Men die face downward,
Women, face upward.

A thousand paper cranes
fill the girl's coffin.

Parents speak
to piles of bones
seeking a lost child.

The dead know best
but have no mouth,
their names float away
on paper lanterns.

Mom's Final Days

"Ralph, I know you work hard,
but you're not a very good farmer."
"I'm not Dad, Mom. Dad's dead.
I'm a college teacher." "Farming
just doesn't pay nowadays. I think
you better quit." "Whatever
you say, Mom." "We've had
quite a dinner this evening.
People from both North and South
were there, but the Southerners
weren't very happy. The war
isn't going very well for them.
I was pleasantly surprised that
they didn't speak as badly as I
thought they would. Very little
slurring of words. Most of them
spoke proper English, so that's
something." "Who do you think
will win the war, Mom?" "Well,
that's a good question, it's touch
and go right now. It snowed
last night and I hope Mother
doesn't slip on the ice." "She's
been dead a long time, Mom."
"My sister, Marie, is going to be
a nurse; my father is a patent
attorney. I think he likes me
better than Mother, because he
takes me places. She lives in
the attic and never comes down."

"There's a lot of movement here
today. Some people are going
to New York and others returning

137

to their country of origin—I don't
know what that is, but I'm sure
the captain of the ship." "You're
in Ohio, Mom." "…has a list,
because he needs to control
the people who come on board.
I'm sure everything will settle down
once the ship has sailed. I'll be glad
to go. I would never send my child
here, it is a very sad place. They
come in and pour water on me,
and laugh about it, as if it were
a joke." "Who does that, Mom?"
"The girls who work here. They
wake me up and pour water
on me." "You mean a shower?"
"Well, you might call it that.
It isn't very scientific. They just
pour water on my head and laugh
about it. It's very sad. I'll be
glad when I get out of here
and go home." "How often
do you have a shower, Mom?"
"Once every few weeks, because
I'm going to marry an officer."

The last time I call Mom says,
"I'm awfully glad to hear from you,
we've just landed and I don't
know anybody." "Landed in what,
Mom?" "It was a flying saucer,
I believe, I can see it parked out
my window. We had a pleasant

fight. Lafayette we are here
for quite a while, so I hope they
take care of us. I don't know what
to expect here, but I'll try to keep
in touch with you, bye-bye."

Mom dies in her sleep
on August 7th, 2006. Her funeral
at her childhood home of Hudson,
Ohio, is attended by a few
friends and family, as well as
a doe and two fawns.

Milking Time

Like his father beside him,
Dad straddles a one-legged stool,
left knee inside the cow's

right hind leg, zinc pail between
his knees, wary of a quick kick
spilling milk or bruising a shin.

Sometimes a sudden swish
of her tail to ward off flies
wraps around his neck,

coarse hairs sting his face.
Though given only easy milkers,
a Holstein with large teats takes

both strong hands for results.
A good cow can fill a pail,
plus free squirts for the eager

cat at his feet. Dad likes
the taste of fresh buttermilk
surfaced with floating globules.

By age twelve he is churning,
raising and lowering a plunger
into cream to agitate it—

a tedious task that takes
a long arm-aching time,
a splashing sound means

the cream has finally broken.
The prized reward: bread,
freshly baked, a clotted cream

spread, a sprinkle of sugar.
When Dad is in his eighties
my wife Roser and I visit

his Florida double-wide,
she hears him wandering about
in the middle of the night,

finds him at the refrigerator
putting butter on bread,
drinking milk from a bottle.

"Don't ever get old," he says.
"I used to do this as a boy.
It helps me sleep."

The Raft

Drifting down the river
the stream moves so slowly
I can see each flower
if I'm looking closely.

Instead I waste my time,
half asleep, half awake,
noting only the slime
curdled along the bank.

When the water widens
into a placid lake
it seems all movement
stops, but that's a mistake.

Remorselessly the stream
rolls on, from slow to fast,
as next white-water rapids
sweep me perilously past

treacherous rocks. Steep falls
drop abruptly to deep
turbulent pools that swirl
until I cannot keep

my balance. And so it
goes, as hours, days, years pass.
I now know with regret
that not one life will last.

About the Author

William Heath was born in Youngstown, Ohio, and grew up in the nearby town of Poland. He has a PhD in American Studies from Case Western Reserve University. During his first teaching job at Kenyon, under the influence of visiting writers Toby Olson and Paul Blackburn, he began writing poems. Later at Transylvania and Vassar he taught American literature and the art of poetry. The best of his early work, gathered in *The Walking Man,* was praised by James Wright: "William Heath is one of the most brilliantly accomplished and gifted young poets to appear in the United States in quite some time. I am especially moved by the delicacy and precision of the language, which indicates as distinguished intelligence, and by the purity and depth of feeling in all of his poems." Richard Wilbur described *The Walking Man* as "a work of a poet how knows how to tell a story."

As a Fulbright at the University of Seville then as a professor at Mount Saint Mary's University, he wrote three novels, an award-winning work of history, and essays on American classics such as Hawthorne, Melville, and Twain. Upon his retirement the William Heath Award was established to honor annually the best student writer. A few years ago he returned to his first love and has since published over a hundred poems; of those gathered in a chapbook, *Night Moves in Ohio,* Kit Hathaway noted that they "are by turns poignant, funny and starkly realistic…teeming with fascinating storyline detail and imagery," while Eamon Grennan added, "These poems are savvy and lively, as exact as a high jumper's focus, quick and accurate as a tennis player's eye, wrist, ankle. *Night Moves in Ohio* is Heath's own remembrance of things past—an autobiography in rapt miniature of his unforgotten early life, mercilessly but compassionately lit by the laser-light of memory."

Steel Valley Elegy includes poems from *Night Moves in Ohio* as well as many more: some depict the civil rights movement in the Deep South and civil disturbances in northern cities. Others present Heath's wry and ironic look at life in these United States, and a final sequence evokes the world of nature while raising philosophical questions. Heath maintains that poetry is written in musical lines about things that matter. His love of language, wide range of interests, and uncanny eye for telling details are always on display. A meditative yet humorous sensibility, an unflinching appetite for reality, memorable eloquence—*Steel Valley Elegy* displays the distinctive skills of an accomplished poet.

williamheathbooks.com